WATCHMAN NEE'S TESTIMONY

Watchman Nee

Living Stream Ministry
Anaheim, California • www.lsm.org

First Edition, November 1991.

ISBN 0-87083-051-1

Published by
Living Stream Ministry
2431 W. La Palma Ave., Anaheim, CA 92801 U.S.A.
P. O. Box 2121, Anaheim, CA 92814 U.S.A.

Printed in the United States of America

01 02 03 04 / 14 13 12 11 10 9 8 7 6

CONTENTS

PREFACE TO THE NEW EDITION

The following is a new edition of the original book *Watchman Nee's Testimony*. The old edition that was first printed in 1974 was somewhat different from the original manuscript. We have secured the original unedited Chinese copy of the manuscript of the compiler, Brother K. H. Weigh, and have retranslated it into English. The result is the following revised edition of the book.

INTRODUCTION

These three testimonies were given by Brother Watchman Nee in a co-workers' meeting held at Kulangsu, an island off the southeastern coast of Fukien province, China, in October 1936. As far as I know, this was the only occasion in his life on which he spoke about his personal affairs in detail. Very seldom had he publicly related his own spiritual experience, probably "lest anyone account of me something above what he sees me to be or hears from me" (2 Cor. 12:6). The testimony which Paul gave in chapter twelve of 2 Corinthians was not publicly divulged until fourteen years later. I have often in the past been thinking of publishing these three testimonies, but in order to share his outlook, I have postponed until now—after the lapse of thirty-seven years. When he died in mainland China on May 30, 1972, I decided to make these testimonies public. I believe this is the right time. I hope that the readers will not pay attention to the person himself, but will pay attention to the work of the Lord in him, and to his willingness in allowing the Lord to perform His work. In this way, the glory of the Lord will be expressed through him. As Paul said, "So that the name of our Lord Jesus may be glorified in you, and you in Him, according to the grace of our God and the Lord Jesus Christ" (2 Thes. 1:12).

The first testimony: Salvation and calling.

The second testimony: (1) Learning the lesson of the cross, (2) Leading in the work, (3) God as my healer, and (4) Four aspects of work entrusted by God.

The third testimony: (1) How to live a life of faith, (2) Attitude towards money, and (3) Looking to God for fulfilling the need of literary work.

These three testimonies by no means comprise the whole of his spiritual life and work before 1936. When we read *The Present Testimony, The Christian* magazine, and open letters published by him before 1936, we can see that there were still a lot of testimonies and work done which were worth mentioning. In that co-workers' meeting, he could not speak more because of the limit of time.

For several years Watchman Nee and I were classmates at Trinity College, a school founded by the Church of England in the city of Foochow. We were good friends and frequently studied and played together. During our junior and senior high school years, we were both nominal Christians. We both had some knowledge of the Bible, and we outwardly kept the Christian forms of baptism, holy communion, church attendance, Bible study, and prayer. But we had never accepted in our hearts the Christ who was crucified for our sins and who resurrected on the third day, and we did not know Him as our personal Savior. We both loved the world and pursued the vanities of the world.

Watchman Nee was pursuing scholastic attainment in the field of Chinese literature. He would frequently write articles for publication in the newspapers. The money he earned was spent on lottery tickets. He was also fond of the movies. I preferred sports and yearned for the fame and praise of men.

In our first college year, his life suddenly changed. He became a fervent Christian and ceased pursuing the world. He frequently testified to his classmates, exhorting them to believe in the Lord Jesus. Many schoolmates did believe in the Lord and began voluntarily to pray in the college chapel, even during weekdays. He would frequently study the Bible in class; however, this did not seem to affect his grades. He usually came out with the highest examination scores in every subject. The lives of many of the students were changed by accepting the Lord, and the dormitory director admitted that some mischievous students, who had previously violated school regulations, had accepted the Lord and experienced a great change in their lives. As a result, he found himself with fewer cases of violation of school rules by students.

Watchman Nee invited me to attend some gospel meetings, but I refused. My heart was set on becoming famous in the sports world. One day, however, he came to my room and preached the gospel to me alone, urging me to accept the Lord Jesus as my Savior. Though I attempted to argue with him concerning some religious problems, he would not argue; instead, he asked me several questions: "Have you sinned? Do you know if your sins are forgiven? Do you know if you are saved?" At the time I didn't understand why, but in my heart I felt sorrowful. Later I realized that this was the convicting work of the Holy Spirit. He preached the gospel to me, explaining that God loved me and gave His only begotten Son for me, and that if I would truly believe in Him, I would not perish but would have eternal life. When asked if I would believe in Christ, I said I would. We knelt together and prayed, with him praying first. Then I prayed, asking the Lord to forgive my sins and thanking Him for loving and saving me. When I rose up, my heart was filled with joy and peace. I experienced a great change in my life and brought forth the fruit of repentance. My name had been one of the names on his prayer list, and the Lord answered his prayer. Praise the Lord!

In 1924 I transferred to Nanking University and came under the influence of modernism. My faith was shaken. At that time Watchman Nee was staying in a brother's home in Nanking, recuperating from an illness. I frequently visited him for fellowship, and he helped me escape the influence of modernism. After his health improved, I was able to make arrangements for him to preach the gospel at Nanking University. As a result of his preaching, two of my classmates were saved.

In 1928, when I was about to leave the university, I considered serving the Lord full-time. I did not want to be a preacher on salary, but I did not know how to live by faith, so I went to Watchman Nee for fellowship. At that time he was quite lonely and greatly in need of co-workers who would be of the same mind. When I raised this matter, he did not encourage me in a careless manner to serve the Lord. He was neither influenced by his need for co-workers nor by the personal relationship between us. He simply told me not to wait until the Jordan waters opened, but to step into the water by faith—then the way would open before me. He knew that I lacked this kind of faith. I was waiting for the outward circumstances to change before beginning to serve the Lord.

(Fifty years ago in China it was difficult to find anyone serving the Lord by faith like Watchman Nee.) Hence, I laid aside the thought of serving the Lord full-time and taught college for eight years.

In the spring of 1934, Watchman Nee held his third overcomer conference in Shanghai. In the morning he spoke on the centrality and universality of Christ. In the afternoon he spoke on God's overcomers. Through his messages in this conference, the Lord gave me revelation which brought about a great turn in my spiritual life. As a result, I stood up in the conference and for the first time consecrated my entire life to the Lord. At that time I was still teaching school.

In 1935 in Chefoo, Brother Nee experienced anew the outpouring of the Holy Spirit. After this, he held a conference in Chuanchow, Fukien, and asked me to attend. There many were helped to experience the outpouring of the Holy Spirit, with the result that they had power and boldness to witness for the Lord. He also preached on the secret of the overcoming life, which is to let Christ live in our stead, according to Paul's testimony in Galatians 2:20. This conference brought in a great revival.

In October 1936, Watchman Nee conducted a co-workers' conference in Kulangsu, Fukien. He cabled me and invited me to attend. By that time I had become clear concerning the Lord's call and was prepared to resign my teaching job to live by faith and serve the Lord. While I was seeking the Lord for His guidance, I received Brother Nee's invitation. I immediately realized that it was the Lord's will for me to attend the conference. I thank the Lord that at this conference I was given the rare opportunity of listening to Watchman Nee's testimony, which I was later able to publish as three articles. At the end of the conference, Brother Nee and the other co-workers assigned me to begin the work in Canton and later in Hong Kong. In 1937 Watchman Nee began the Lord's work in the southwest part of China in the city of K'un-ming in Yunnan province. After establishing the church there, he invited me to come and work in that locality. I picked up the burden and moved my family there. I worked there for three years, until my return to Hong Kong in 1940.

Following World War II, whenever Watchman Nee visited Canton or Hong Kong, I took the opportunity to seek his fellowship. I usually planned to ask him a number of questions, but after having some fellowship with him, it was unnecessary to ask the questions. In our fellowship I always received an abundant supply of life.

In 1948 I again had opportunity to attend a conference in the church in Shanghai. Brother Nee ministered on the matter of handing over ourselves with all we possess to the Lord. His words were full of impact and the power of the Holy Spirit, and the meetings were full of the Lord's presence. Many were revived and handed over themselves and their possessions, to be built together in serving the Lord. In the last meeting of the conference, because I was leaving for Foochow, Brother Nee, in the presence of all the assembled brothers and sisters, addressed me in the following words of farewell:

There is only one Christ, but due to different viewpoints and emphases of the workers, it seems that Christ has been divided into many Christs. If a worker cannot express to others the one Christ whom God desires to present, his work is a failure. Many today have had very intimate contact with the Lord, while others are merely pressing against Him (Mark 5:24). Perhaps some have indeed touched His back, held His hand, or torn His garments; yet they have no relationship whatever with Him in life. Among the many who thronged Jesus, the woman with an issue of blood was not the only one who was ill, but she was the only one healed in life (Matt. 9:20-22).

Some today indeed know the Christ of Bethsaida (Mark 8:22-26) or the Christ of Gadara (Mark 5:1-20) or the Christ of Emmaus (Luke 24:13-35). In their experience they have really seen the miracles and the wonders. They may even be able to perform the miracles themselves. Yet if there is no true inward revelation, none of these works will amount to anything. Some may be able to tell others with moving power of a Christ of Emmaus. They may be able to expound the Scriptures and may cause others to become truly fervent in their hearts; yet it is all to no avail. The real work is to impart a Christ of revelation to others. I speak these words not only to Brother Weigh, but to all the co-workers and to all the brothers and sisters alike. If you and I cannot impart a Christ of revelation to others, our work is a failure.

Here we see that there are two basically different stands that a worker of the Lord can take: one emphasizes work, the expounding of the Scriptures, miracles, works of wonders, and answers to prayers, etc. The other presents before men a Christ of revelation.

In the same year, 1948, from the beginning of June to the end of September, Watchman Nee held a period of training on Mount Kuling, Fukien, for the purpose of training co-workers from all over China. I attended that training. Every day we spent approximately seven hours listening to Brother Nee and receiving his ministry. I was greatly helped in my spiritual understanding and also in the principles of working for the Lord. What he spoke at the training sessions may be summarized as follows:

(1) How to exercise our spirit.
(2) How to be a minister of the Word.
(3) How to read the Bible.
(4) How to preach the gospel.
(5) How to guide new believers.
(6) How to manage church affairs.

There were also meetings for testimonies, in which the participants gave brief testimonies. Then Brother Nee made a spiritual diagnosis of each person's testimony, pointing out each one's spiritual difficulties and the way to be delivered from them. With a keen feeling, he diagnosed accurately so that what he pointed out exactly met the needs of each person. When the co-workers went back to their respective local churches after coming down from the mountain, the Lord abundantly blessed the churches, bringing about enormous revival so that the churches were built up and there was progress in the work, with the result that the gospel was being preached with power, enabling many people to be saved.

In the early part of 1950, Watchman Nee came to Hong Kong. Soon Witness Lee also joined him. In the past it had been a rare occurrence for these two brothers to visit the same church at the same time. Their ministry issued in a great revival in the church in Hong Kong. Previously there had been about three hundred in the meetings. As a result of the revival the number increased to between two and three thousand. There was a special blessing upon the church in Hong Kong.

Soon Brother Nee contemplated going back to Shanghai. The political situation there being then extremely tense, the brothers tried to persuade him not to return to mainland China, but he insisted on doing so, as he was concerned about the churches and co-workers there. He was like the apostle Paul who, on the eve of going to Jerusalem, knew that imprisonment and hardships awaited him there and was ready even to die for the name of the Lord Jesus. On account of his love for the Lord, for the church, and for the brothers and sisters, he was in the same frame of mind as Paul. During the first year or two after returning to Shanghai, he availed himself of every opportunity to put his heart and soul into the work diligently. There were then over six hundred local churches throughout the country with over ninety thousand saints, most of whom had received assistance from him in some way. In 1952, on account of his loyalty to the Lord and for the sake of the truth, Brother Nee was unexpectedly arrested and put in jail, being sentenced to twenty years' imprisonment. In those twenty years it was impossible to get direct news about him. As far as I know, the government made use of him by making him translate scientific books from English into Chinese. His wife, who died before him in November 1971, used to visit him once every two or three weeks and bring him some daily necessities. Brother Nee's heart was only half as big as a normal person's, and he had been suffering from heart disease for many years, causing him acute pain during fits of illness. However, the Lord preserved his life until May 30, 1972, when he was taken up by the Lord into His bosom for rest. Brother Nee thus rested from his labors, and his works do follow him

(Rev. 14:13). Although his physical body was confined in prison, the messages which the Lord had imparted to him are being widely spread without any restriction throughout the whole world. By virtue of the ministry of his words, many saints have had spiritual insight through revelation, the churches have been built up, and many items of truths hitherto hidden in the Bible have been uncovered. Such books as Brother Nee's *Normal Christian Life* and *Normal Christian Church Life* are in great demand in America and Europe and have enabled many people to be enlightened and greatly changed in their spiritual life, thus returning to the ground of unity in local churches and bearing good testimonies. The messages spoken and the work done by God through him in the past half century have been extremely numerous and abundant. These three testimonies are but a small part of the happenings before 1936. What I have narrated in respect to things which happened between 1928 and 1952 is also very brief. From his many books we may notice how clear was our brother's understanding of God and how he dedicated himself; in loyalty and obedience he was willing even to accept death. He was indeed a vessel much used by God, and, "having served his own generation by the counsel of God, did indeed fall asleep" (Acts 13:36). He has, indeed, also left "you a model so that you may follow in His steps" (1 Pet. 2:21). May the Lord bless these three testimonies so that each reader will "remember the ones leading you, who have spoken to you the word of God; and considering the issue of their manner of life, imitate their faith" (Heb. 13:7). To our God and the Lord Jesus be glory for evermore! Amen.

Kwang-hsi Weigh
the compiler

CHAPTER ONE

THE FIRST TESTIMONY—
SALVATION AND CALLING
GIVEN ON OCTOBER 18, 1936

Scripture Reading: Acts 26:29; Gal. 1:15

FAMILY BACKGROUND

I was born into a Christian family. I was the third child preceded by two sisters. Because I had an aunt who had borne six daughters in succession, my paternal aunt was displeased when my mother bore two girls. According to Chinese custom, males are preferred over females. When my mother gave birth to two girls, people said she would probably be like my aunt, bearing half a dozen girls before bringing forth a boy. Though at that time my mother was not clearly saved, she knew how to pray. So she spoke to the Lord, saying, "If I have a boy, I will present him to You." The Lord heard her prayer and I was born. My father told me, "Before you were born, your mother promised to present you to the Lord."

SAVED AND CALLED AT THE SAME TIME

I was saved in 1920 at the age of seventeen. Before being saved I experienced some mental conflict concerning whether or not to accept the Lord Jesus as my Savior and whether or not to become the Lord's servant. For most people, the problem at the time of salvation is how to be delivered from sin. But for me, being saved from sin and my life career were linked together. If I were to accept the Lord Jesus as my Savior, I would simultaneously accept Him as my Lord. He would deliver me not only from sin but also from the world. At that time I was afraid of being saved, for I knew that once I was saved I must serve the Lord. Of necessity, therefore, my salvation would be a dual salvation. It was impossible for me to set aside the Lord's calling and to desire only salvation. I had to choose either to believe in the Lord and have a dual salvation or forfeit both. For me to accept the Lord would mean that both events would take place simultaneously.

FINAL DECISION

On the evening of April 29, 1920, I was alone in my room. I had no peace of mind. Whether I sat or reclined, I could find no rest, for within was this problem of whether or not I should believe in the Lord. My first inclination was not to believe in the Lord Jesus and not to be a Christian. However, that made me inwardly uneasy. There was a real struggle within me. Then I knelt down to pray. At first I had no words with which to pray. But eventually many sins came before me, and I realized that I was a sinner. I had never had such an experience in my life before that time. I saw myself as a sinner and I also saw the Savior. I saw the filthiness of sin and I also saw the efficacy of the Lord's precious blood cleansing me and making me white as snow. I saw the Lord's hands nailed to the cross, and at the same time I saw Him stretching forth His arms to welcome me, saying, "I am here waiting to receive you." Overwhelmed by such love, I could not possibly reject it, and I decided to accept Him as my Savior. Previously, I had laughed at those who believed in the Lord, but that evening I could not laugh. Instead, I wept and confessed my sins, seeking the Lord's forgiveness. After making my confession, the burden of sins was discharged, and I felt buoyant and full of inward joy and peace. This was the first time in my life that I knew I was a sinner. I prayed for the first time and had my first experience of joy and peace. There might have been some joy and peace before, but the experience after my salvation was very real. Alone in my room that evening, I saw the light and lost all consciousness of my surroundings. I said to the Lord, "Lord, You have really been gracious to me."

GIVING UP MY FUTURE

In this audience there are at least three schoolmates of mine. Among them is Brother Weigh Kwang-hsi, who can testify concerning what an ill-behaved student I was, as well as what a wonderful student I was in school. On the evil side, I often violated the school rules. On the good side, I was always first in every examination, because God had bestowed intelligence on me. My essays were frequently posted on the bulletin board for exhibition. At that time I was a youth with many grand dreams and many plans for the future. I considered my judgments sound. I can humbly say that had I worked hard in the world, it would have been quite possible for me to have had great success. My schoolmates can also testify to this. But following my salvation many new things happened to me. All my previous planning became void and was brought to nothing. My future career was entirely abandoned. For some this step might be easy, but for me, with many ideals, dreams, and plans, it was exceedingly difficult. From the evening I was saved, I began to live a new life, for the life of the eternal God had entered into me.

My salvation and calling to serve the Lord took place simultaneously. Since that evening, I have never once had any doubts about being called. During that hour I decided on my future career once and for all. I realized that, on the one hand, the Lord had saved me for my sake, and at the same time, He did so for His own sake. He wanted me to obtain His eternal life, and He also wanted me to serve Him and be His co-worker. As a boy I did not understand the nature of preaching. When I was older, I considered it the most trifling and base of occupations. In those days most preachers were employed by European or American missionaries. They were servile subordinates to the missionaries and earned merely eight or nine dollars per month. I had no intention of becoming a preacher nor even a Christian. I could never have imagined that I would choose the profession of a preacher, a profession which I despised and considered trifling and base.

LEARNING TO SERVE THE LORD

After being saved, I continued on in school, though I had little interest in books. Others read novels in class, but I diligently studied the Bible. [Editor's note: Although Brother

Nee studied the Bible in class, he still came first in the end-of-term examinations.] Later, desiring to pursue spiritual things further, I left school and entered Dora Yu's Bible Institute in Shanghai [Editor's note: a famous lady evangelist]. However, before long she politely dismissed me, and I returned home. The reason she gave for her action was that it was inconvenient for me to stay there any longer. I realized that my flesh had not been dealt with. I was still fond of good food and fine clothing, and I enjoyed sleeping until eight o'clock in the morning. Dora Yu felt I was good material for the Lord's interest and had good prospects, but when she discovered my laziness, she sent me home.

At that time I was thoroughly disappointed and felt my future was doomed. At that time I even questioned my salvation. But surely I was saved! I even considered that I was quite good and that I had been transformed in many ways, not realizing that there was much yet to be learned and much to be dealt with. Confident that the Lord had saved me and called me, I could not be disappointed. I admitted that I was not yet good enough, but I felt that with the passing of more time I would improve.

Since the time was not ripe for me to continue my spiritual pursuits, I decided to return to school. When my schoolmates saw me, they recognized that I had changed, but I had not changed thoroughly, for I still occasionally lost my temper and did some things wrong. There were times when I seemed very much like a saved person, but at other times I seemed very much like an unsaved person. Therefore, my testimony in the school was not very powerful, and when I witnessed to Brother Weigh, he paid no heed. [Editor's note: Brother Nee's prayers and guidance finally brought Brother Weigh to the Lord.]

After I was saved, I spontaneously loved the souls of sinners and hoped that they would be saved. To this end, I began to preach the gospel and to bear testimony among my schoolmates. After nearly a year's work, however, no one was saved. I thought the more words I could speak and the more reasons I could present, the more effective I would be in saving people. But though I had much to speak concerning the Lord, my words lacked power to move the listeners.

Prayer for Others' Salvation

About this time I met a Western missionary, Miss Groves (Margaret Barber's co-worker), who asked me how many persons I had brought to the Lord in the year following my salvation. I bowed my head, hoping to forestall further questioning, and shamefully admitted in a low voice that, although I had preached the gospel to my schoolmates, they did not like to listen, and when they did listen, they would not believe. My attitude was that, since they would not heed the gospel, they would have to bear the consequences. She spoke to me frankly, "You are unable to lead people to the Lord because there is something between God and you. It may be some hidden sins not yet completely dealt with, or something for which you are indebted to someone." I admitted that such things existed, and she asked if I were willing to settle them immediately. I answered that I was willing.

She also asked how I went about bearing testimony. I replied that I pulled people in at random and began to speak, regardless of whether they were listening or not. She said, "This is not right. You must speak to God first, before you speak to people. You should pray to God, make a list of your schoolmates' names, and ask God which of them you should pray for. Pray for them daily, mentioning them by name. Then when God affords the opportunity, you should bear testimony to them."

After that conversation, I immediately began to deal with my sins by making restitution, paying debts, being reconciled with my schoolmates, and confessing offenses to others. I also entered in my notebook the names of about seventy schoolmates and began praying for them daily, mentioning their names individually before God. Sometimes I prayed for them once every hour, praying silently, even in class. When opportunity arose, I would bear testimony to them and try to persuade them to believe in the Lord Jesus. My schoolmates often said jokingly, "Mr. Preacher is coming. Let us listen to his preaching." The fact was that they had no intention to listen.

I called on Miss Groves again and said to her, "I have fully carried out your instructions. Why is it not effective?" She replied, "Do not be disappointed. Keep praying until some are saved." By the Lord's grace, I continued to pray daily. When opportunity arose, I bore testimony and preached the gospel. Thank the Lord, after several months, all but one of the seventy persons whose names were in my notebook were saved.

To Be Filled with the Holy Spirit

Though some had been saved, I was still not satisfied, because many in the school and in the town were still not saved. I felt the need to be filled with the Holy Spirit and to receive power from above that I might be able to bring more people to the Lord. Then I called on Miss Margaret Barber. Being immature in spiritual matters, I asked her if it was necessary to be filled with the Holy Spirit in order to obtain power to bring many to salvation. She answered, "Yes." I asked her concerning the means to be filled with the Holy Spirit. She said, "You must present yourself to God that He may fill you with Himself." I replied that I had already presented myself. But when I considered, I knew that I was still my old self. I knew that God had saved me, chosen me, and called me. Though I had not yet attained absolute victory, I had been freed from sins and evil habits, and many matters hitherto entangling me had been abandoned. However, I still felt the lack of spiritual power to cope with spiritual work. Then she told me the following story:

Brother Prigin was an American who had been to China. He had obtained a master's degree and was studying for a Ph.D. Feeling the condition of his spiritual life unsatisfactory, he sought the Lord and prayed. He said to God, "I have very strong unbelief; some sins I cannot overcome, and I have no power to work." For two weeks he asked God specifically to fill him with the Holy Spirit that he might lead a victorious life with power. God said, "Do you really want this? If so, do not take the Ph.D. examination two months from now, for I have no need of a doctor of philosophy." He felt he was in a dilemma. The Ph.D. degree seemed a sure thing; it would be a pity not to sit for the examination. He knelt down to pray and ask why God would not allow him to get the degree and be a minister as well. But here is a strange thing: Once God has made a demand, He sticks to it and never compromises with anyone.

The following two months were most painful. On the last Saturday of that period he experienced real conflict within. Did he want the degree or did he want to be filled with the Holy Spirit? Which was better: a doctor's degree or a victorious life? Others could be doctors and yet be used by God as well—why couldn't he? He was struggling and reasoning with God and was at his wits' end. The Ph.D. was dear to him and so was the filling of the Holy Spirit. But God would not give way. To choose a doctor's degree would make it impossible to live the spiritual life. To live the spiritual life would require forfeiting a doctor's degree. At length, with tears in his eyes, he said, "I submit. Despite my two years' study toward a Ph.D. degree, a goal which I have cherished for thirty years, ever since childhood, I have no alternative but to relinquish sitting for the examination for the sake of submission to God." Following this decision he wrote to notify the university authorities that he would not sit for the examination on Monday, thus abandoning hope for a Ph.D. degree once and for all. He was so exhausted that night that he could find no message to deliver the following day. So he simply told the congregation the story of his surrender to the Lord. On that day the congregation was revived. Three-quarters of them were in tears. He himself also gained strength. He said, "If I had known before that the result would be like this, I would have submitted earlier." His subsequent work was greatly blessed by the Lord, and he was one who had the deepest knowledge of God.

When I visited England, I intended to go on to the United States to meet him, but the Lord took him before I had the opportunity. But when I heard this testimony, I said to the Lord, "I am willing to remove anything standing between God and me in order to be filled with the Holy Spirit." Between 1920 and 1922 I went to at least two or three hundred people to confess offenses. After a further strict scrutiny of past events, I felt there was still something between God and me; otherwise, I would have had spiritual vitality. But despite further dealings in many ways, I still could not gain strength.

DEALT WITH BY GOD

One day while seeking a theme from the Bible before delivering a message, I randomly opened the Bible and Psalm 73:25 appeared before my eyes: "Whom have I in heaven but thee? And there is none upon earth that I desire besides thee." After reading these words I said to myself, "The writer of this psalm can say that, but I cannot." I discovered then that there was something between me and God.

Since my wife is not present today, I will relate the story to you. About ten years before our marriage, I was in love with her. She was not then saved, and when I spoke with her about the Lord Jesus and tried to persuade her to believe, she laughed at me. I must admit that I did love her, but at the same time I suffered her laughter at the Lord I believed in. I also questioned at that time whether she or the Lord would have first place in my heart. I must say that once young people have fallen in love, they find it very difficult to give up their beloved. I told God of my willingness to give her up, but deep in my heart I was not willing. After reading Psalm 73 again, I said to God, "I cannot say that there is none upon earth that I desire besides Thee, because there is one on earth whom I love." At that instant, the Holy Spirit indicated clearly that there was something between God and me.

On that day I delivered a message, but I did not know what I was talking about. I was actually speaking to God, asking Him to be patient and impart strength to me until I could give her up. I asked God to postpone dealing with this matter. But God never reasons with people. I considered going to the frontier of desolate Tibet to evangelize and suggested many other enterprises to God, hoping that He might be moved not to raise again the question of my giving up the one I loved. But once God's finger has pointed to something, He will not withdraw it. No matter how hard I prayed, I could not get through. I had no enthusiasm for my studies in school, and at the same time I failed to acquire the power of the Holy Spirit, which I was earnestly seeking. I was in great distress. I prayed constantly, hoping that my earnest supplication might change God's mind. Thank the Lord that all along He wanted me to learn to deny myself, to lay aside human love, and love Him with a single heart. Otherwise, I would be a useless Christian in His hand. He cut down my natural life with a sharp knife so that I might learn a lesson which I had never learned before.

On one occasion I delivered a message and returned to my room with a heavy heart. I told God that I would return to school the following Monday and seek for the filling of the Holy Spirit and the love of Christ. During the following two weeks, I found that I still could not say with conviction the words of Psalm 73:25. But thank the Lord, soon afterwards I was filled with His love, and I was willing to lay my loved one down and loudly declare, "I will lay her aside! Never will she be mine!" After this declaration I was at long last able to utter the words of Psalm 73:25. On that day I was in the second heaven, if not the third. The world appeared smaller to me, and it was as if I were mounting the clouds and riding the mists. On the evening of my salvation, the burden of my sins rolled away, but on that day, February 13, 1922, when I laid aside my beloved, my heart was emptied of everything that previously occupied me.

In the following week, people began to be saved. Brother Weigh, who was my classmate, can testify to the fact that up to this time I had been very particular about my dress. I used to wear a long silk gown with red dots. But on that day, I removed my refined clothing and shoes. I went to the kitchen, made some paste, and with a bundle of gospel posters in my arms, went to the street to post them on the walls and to distribute gospel tracts. In those days in Foochow, Fukien, this was a pioneer act.

From my second school term in 1922, I began the gospel work, and many of my schoolmates were saved. I prayed daily for those whose names were in my notebook. From 1923, we began to borrow or rent places for meetings to expand the work of evangelization. Several hundred people were saved at the same time. All but one of those whose names were in my notebook were saved. This is evident proof that God listens to such prayers. It is His way that we must first pray for sinners before they can be saved. In those few years there were many instances to confirm this fact.

LEARNING THE LESSON OF SUBMISSION

In 1923 seven of us worked together as co-workers. Two of us took the lead, a co-worker who was five years my senior and myself. We had a co-workers' meeting every Friday in which the other five were often forced to listen to the arguing between the leading two. We were all young then, and each had his own way of thinking. I often charged the elder co-worker with being wrong, and vice versa. Since my temperament had not been dealt with, I frequently lost my temper. Today in 1936 I do sometimes laugh, but I seldom laughed at that time. In our controversies I admit that many times I was wrong, but he was also at times in the wrong. It was easy for me to forgive my own faults, but not easy to forgive others. After having a dispute on Friday, I would go to Sister Barber on Saturday and accuse the other co-worker. I would say, "I told that co-worker that he should act in a certain way, but he would not listen. You should speak to him." Sister Barber replied, "He is five years older than you; you should listen to him and obey him." I answered, "Am I to listen to him whether he is reasonable or not?" She said, "Yes! The Scriptures say that the younger should obey the elder." I replied, "I cannot possibly do this. A Christian should act according to reason." She answered, "Whether there is reason or not, you need not care. The Scriptures say that the younger should obey the elder." I was angry at heart that the

Bible would say such a thing. I wanted to give vent to my indignation, but I could not.

Each time following the controversy on Friday, I would go to her to state my grievances, but she would again quote the Scriptures, demanding that I obey the elder. Sometimes I wept Friday evening after the dispute on Friday afternoon. Then I would go to Sister Barber the next day to state my grievances, hoping that she would vindicate me. But I would weep again after coming home Saturday evening. I wished I had been born a few years earlier. In one controversy I had very good arguments. I felt that when I pointed them out, she would see how my co-worker was wrong and would support me. But she said, "Whether that co-worker is wrong or not is another matter. While you are accusing your brother before me, are you like one who is bearing the cross? Are you like a lamb?" When she questioned me in this way, I felt very ashamed and I could never forget it. My speech and my attitude that day revealed that I was indeed not like one bearing the cross, nor like a lamb.

In such circumstances I learned to obey an elder co-worker. In that year and a half, I learned the most precious lesson in my life. My head was filled with ideas, but God wanted to see me enter into spiritual reality. In that year and a half, I came to realize what it is to bear the cross. Today in 1936 we have some fifty co-workers. Had it not been for the lesson of obedience which I learned in that year and a half, I fear that I could not work together with anyone. God put me in those circumstances that I might learn to be under the restraint of the Holy Spirit. In those eighteen months I had no opportunity to put forward my proposals. I could only weep and painfully suffer. But had it not been for this, I would never have realized how difficult it was for me to be dealt with. God wanted to polish me and to remove all my sharp, projecting edges. This has been a difficult thing to accomplish. How I thank and praise God, whose grace has brought me through!

Now I must speak a word to the young co-workers. If you cannot stand the trials of the cross, you cannot become a useful instrument. It is only the spirit of a lamb that God

takes delight in: the gentleness, the humility, and the peace.
Your ambition, lofty purpose, and ability are all useless in
the sight of God. I have been down this path and must often
confess my shortcomings. All that pertains to me is in the
hand of God. It is not a question of right or wrong; it is a
question of whether or not one is like the bearer of the cross.
In the church, right and wrong have no place; all that counts
is bearing the cross and accepting its breaking. This produces
the overflowing of God's life and accomplishes His will.

CHAPTER TWO

THE SECOND TESTIMONY—
GIVEN ON OCTOBER 20, 1936

Today I want to testify concerning four things: (1) learning
the lesson of the cross, (2) leading in the work, (3) receiving
healing to my sickness and experiencing God as my Healer,
and (4) four aspects of work entrusted by the Lord.

LEARNING THE LESSON OF THE CROSS

A believer may read, study, or expound a teaching
concerning the cross, while at the same time not necessarily
receive the lesson of the cross or know the way of the cross.
When I was being tempered together in the service with my
co-workers, the Lord ordered many crosses for me. Many
times I felt embarrassed. I would not accept the dealing of
the cross and found it difficult to submit. Inwardly, however,
I knew that if the cross were ordered by the Lord, it would
be the right thing, though it would still be difficult to obey
and accept it. While the Lord was on the earth, He learned
obedience by the cross which He suffered (Heb. 5:8; Phil. 2:8).
How could I be an exception? In the first eight or nine months,
when the lesson of the cross began to come, I would not obey.
I knew that I should yield without resistance to the cross
ordered by the Lord. When I would make up my mind to obey,
my determination would last only a short time. When some
event would arise where I should obey, I found it difficult to
obey and was full of rebellious thoughts. This made me very
uneasy.

Once I recognized the cross which the Lord had ordered
for me, I found it very beneficial. Among my co-workers, five
had been my schoolmates since childhood. Another one came
from a different city and was five years older than I. The five
always sided with him and opposed me. No matter what I
did, they would invariably condemn me. They received the

credit for many things I did. Sometimes when they rejected my views, I went to a lonely hill to cry before God. At these times I wrote some hymns on bearing the cross. For the first time I experienced the significance of "the fellowship of His sufferings" (Phil. 3:10). When I could not have fellowship with the world, I could enjoy heavenly fellowship. The first two years after my salvation, I did not know what the cross was. But at this time I was beginning to learn its lesson.

I was always ranked first in my class as well as in my school. I also wanted to be first in serving the Lord. For this reason, when I was made second, I disobeyed. I told God repeatedly that it was too much for me to bear; I was receiving too little honor and authority, and everyone sided with my elder co-worker. But today I worship God and thank Him from the depths of my heart that this all happened to me. It has been the best training. God wished me to learn obedience, so He arranged for me to encounter many difficulties. Eventually, I told Him I was willing to be placed second. When I became willing to yield, the joy I experienced differed from the joy I experienced at the time of my salvation; it was not a broad joy but a deep one. After another eight or nine months, on many occasions I was willing to be broken and did not do what I wished. On my spiritual path I was filled with joy and peace. The Lord submitted to the hand of God, and I was willing to do the same. The Lord, existing in the form of God, did not consider being equal with God a treasure to be grasped, but emptied Himself (Phil. 2:6-7). How dare I rank myself above the Lord? When I first began to learn obedience it was difficult, but as time went on I found it easier and easier. Eventually, I told God that I would choose the cross, accept its breaking, and put aside my own ideas.

LEADING IN THE WORK

When God's work started in several places in China in 1921, some truths were not clearly distinguished. For instance, grace and law were not clearly defined; nor were the kingdom of heaven and eternal life, grace and reward, or salvation and victory clearly differentiated. The understanding of truths in the Lord was neither deep nor rich enough. However, the understanding of the gospel of grace was comparatively clear, and it was being quite clearly preached at that time when Mr. Wang Ming-dao was in Teh-Chow, Sister Pearl Wang and Ruth Lee were in Nanking, and some other workers and I were in Foochow.

Publishing *The Present Testimony*

By the end of 1922 I had a burden to publish a magazine, because a number had been saved in Foochow, and the number was increasing. At that time, Brother Leland Wang was away in the Yangtze region doing evangelistic work. Only his wife and children were at home. He asked me to move into his house to help take care of the family. Daily, Sister Wang and I prayed for the magazine. I was at that time extremely pressed financially. After praying for more than a month, there was not a single dollar on hand. One morning I arose and said, "There is no need to pray further—that would be a lack of faith. What I must do is start writing. God need not put the money into our hands before we begin to write! Henceforth, I will no longer pray for this matter, but will proceed with the preparation of drafts."

When everything was ready and the last word had been written, I said, "Now the money will come." Eventually, I knelt down to pray again, saying, "O God, the draft is ready for printing, but there is still no money." After praying thus, I felt wonderfully confident that God would certainly give the money. We began to praise God.

The amazing thing was that we had no more risen to our feet than there was a knock at the door. I thought someone was coming with the money. That house being Sister Wang's, I let her answer the door. To my surprise, the one who came was a wealthy yet stingy sister. "Oh, since it is she," I thought, "there could be no money." But she said to me, "I have something extremely important to see you about." "Please tell me," I replied. Then she asked, "How should a Christian donate?" I replied that we should not adopt the Old Testament way of paying tithes, but follow the word in 2 Corinthians 9:7, which says that each person should give according to the order of God. He may donate a half, a third, a tenth, or a twentieth of his income. She then asked, "Where should the donation be made?" I answered, "Do not give it to a church which opposes the Lord, nor to those who do not believe the Bible or the redemption of the Lord's shed blood. If no one contributes to them, they will not be able to carry on their preaching. Pray before each donation; then give it either to the poor or to some work, but never to an improper organization." She said, "The Lord has been speaking to me for many days concerning my excessive devotion to money. At first I could not reconcile myself to this, but now I can do so. When I was praying this morning, the Lord said to me, 'There is no need for you to pray anymore. Just start giving away your money.' I was rather disconcerted, but now I am here with thirty dollars for you to use for the Lord's work." This money was just sufficient for the printing of fourteen hundred copies of *The Present Testimony*. Later, another person gave an additional thirty dollars, which was sufficient for the postage and incidental expenses. This is how the first issue of *The Present Testimony* was published.

The Beginning of Revival

At the beginning of 1923, we started to hold meetings in Foochow in a pavilion of a brother's house. Stools were collected from various places when needed, and we went about the neighborhood inviting people to come and listen. Because the Lord had started something, it was easy for many people to be saved. Our method of inviting people was rather effective: each brother wore a white vest bearing words like "You shall die" in the front and "Believe in Jesus to be saved" at the back. There were other similar slogans. With banners in our hands, we paraded everywhere, singing as we marched along the way. Those who saw us marveled, and in this way, many people were brought to the meeting. We marched this way every day, and every day people came to listen to the gospel. They filled the sitting room, the kitchen, and outside the pavilion.

We had rented some stools for the meeting, but the rental period expired after two weeks. When the time was up, we had no money. The stools had to be returned to the owner. Must the meeting be suspended? I announced that anybody who wished to attend the meeting in the future would have to bring his own stool. That afternoon, the whole hill, Tsang Chien Hill, was the scene of people, old and young, boys and girls, carrying stools. Even the policemen were amazed at the sight.

Thank the Lord, through His special blessing, a few hundred people were saved. On that occasion the foundation of salvation was laid down clearly. Until that time, many believers in China had not been clear about salvation. It was through those meetings and the preaching of our brothers in various places that many have since come to understand it.

Renting Premises for the Meeting

After we had been holding meetings for about a month, some young brothers among us felt that we should have a proper place to meet in the future. But since we were short of money, it was beyond our means to do so. I went to school to talk the matter over with several brothers, that is, with brothers Faithful Luke, Simon Meek, and Wang Tsi, and we agreed that we should continue our work among the students. Then for the first time I rented some premises, a place owned by a family named Ho, all the members of which had been saved. They agreed to rent the place to me for a monthly amount of only nine dollars. I then prayed with several brothers, asking God to supply the three months' rent which was needed in advance before we could move in.

Every Saturday I went to Ma-Kiang, Fukien, to listen to Miss Margaret Barber's preaching. This time when I saw her, she said, "Here is twenty-seven dollars, which a friend asked me to give you for your work." This sum was exactly sufficient for three months' rent at nine dollars per month—not too much and not too little. On my return, without hesitation, I paid the three months' rent in advance. Later, we prayed again, and the Lord provided again. This was the beginning of the work in Foochow.

The Revival of Many Believers

I have never seen a revival greater than this one. At that time, there were people being saved every day. It looked as if anyone who contacted us would immediately be saved. Every morning at five o'clock, when I arrived at school, I saw people everywhere reading the Bible—more than one hundred of them. Reading novels had been very fashionable, but now those who wanted to could only do so secretly. Instead, Bible reading now became an honorable thing to do. There were eight classes in our school, each with a prefect and a deputy prefect. It was amazing to see that the prefect of practically every class had been saved. Even all the famous athletes had been saved, among whom was Brother Weigh Kwang-hsi, the tennis champion of Fukien province for many years. Our headmaster admired us for everything we did. The only thing he lamented was our attitude towards the Anglican church. The headmaster was a member of the Anglican church, but we refused to belong to that denomination.

More than sixty people daily marched in procession carrying banners, and a few dozen also went around daily distributing tracts. The whole town of Foochow—about a hundred thousand people—was shaken.

Many brothers who were saved were immediately baptized. At this time, we began to meet according to the Scripture. This was the way the meeting in Foochow started. Later the number of believers increased, and the work in the villages also began.

A New Beginning in the Work

During the period between 1921 and 1923, revival meetings were held to lead people to the Lord. At that time preaching the gospel was believed to be the unique work for God. But God opened my eyes to see that His purpose requires that those who have been saved by grace stand upon the ground of oneness in local churches to represent and maintain God's testimony on earth. Some of my co-workers had different views of the truth concerning the church. But when I carefully studied the book of Acts, I realized that God's wish is to establish local churches in every city. At that time the light shone upon me so clearly that I recognized that this is His purpose.

At the same time I received this light, a problem arose with some co-workers who held different views regarding important points of our work. This resulted in friction among us. They felt that we should be zealous in revival and gospel preaching work and that the fruit of such work could be easily seen. My view, however, was to establish local churches with less stress on the revival and preaching side. When an older co-worker went out to hold gospel meetings, as he frequently did, I was at times tempted to secretly hold revival gospel meetings of my own. However, instead of doing this, when he was away, I immediately acted according to the vision I had received. Upon his return, he would undo what I had done and work according to his concept. But when he was again absent, I would go back to my previous way. Consequently, we oscillated back and forth on this matter all the time. Since the light each of us had received in respect to the work was different, our ways of working were also different. One way was that of revival and evangelism, while the other way was that of establishing local churches. What the Lord revealed to me was extremely clear: Before long He would raise up local churches in various parts of China. Whenever I closed my eyes, the vision of the birth of local churches appeared. [Editor's note: By 1949, there were about four to five hundred local churches being raised up all over China.]

In 1924, some workers were not satisfied with me, and God suffered the church in Foochow to be suddenly brought to a test. In order to avert a split, I then left Foochow. Later there was a call to visit Southeast Asia; so I went there, and meetings were also started there. In May 1925 I returned and rented premises in Pagoda, Foochow, a small village near the sea, with the aim of settling down. At this time I felt that we should publish a magazine laying stress on the truths concerning salvation and the church and also touching upon prophecy and types. My original intention for this magazine, known as *The Christian,* was that it should be of only a temporary nature. In 1925 two issues were published, in 1926, ten, and because of continuous demand, twelve in 1927.

In the first half of 1926, I visited Amoy, Kulangsu, Changchow, and Tung-An to bear testimony, and many people were saved. In the second half of the year, I went back to those places. This time I was very tired as I had to conduct meetings, write articles, and attend to correspondence as well. I was then already slightly indisposed. I was originally scheduled to have ten days of meetings, but on the ninth day I fell ill. Another worker came and resumed the work for a few more days. It was in the second half of 1926 that the work in the south of Fukien started, with meetings in Amoy, Tung-An, and the neighboring districts.

Some doctors said that the disease I had contracted while in Amoy was probably fatal and that I could expect to live only a few months! I was not afraid of death but I could not help thinking of what I had learned from the Lord during the many years before and the lessons I had experienced, none of which had yet been put into writing. Surely all this ought not to go with me to the grave! I prepared to write *The Spiritual Man.*

When I arrived in Nanking, I learned that a number of brothers and sisters who were standing on the ground of unity in the local church broke bread together, so naturally I went to them and joined them in remembrance of the Lord. Brother Weigh Kwang-hsi, a schoolmate of mine, was then studying at the University of Nanking. Through his introduction I went to the university to deliver several sermons, at the same time regaining two brothers, whom we accepted at the Lord's table. This was the beginning of our work in Nanking.

In order to be able to devote myself to the writing of *The Spiritual Man,* I soon left Nanking and went to the country in Wusih, where I wrote the first four sections. There was military action in Nanking in March 1927, and as it was impossible to communicate with brothers and sisters at some places, I left the countryside for Shanghai. On arriving I learned that many brothers and sisters had been arriving one after another from different places. Prior to my arrival in Shanghai, there had been bread-breaking meetings in Sister Pearl Wang's house at Hsin's Garden. After we had all arrived, our meeting place was moved to Keng Ching Lane, and the Gospel Bookroom was started in Shanghai.

Toward the end of 1927, we had a prayer meeting every day. The believers in and around Ping-Yang, north of the Yangtze River, who had been helped by our written testimonies, began to correspond with us. Realizing that they were ready for instruction and that the believers in China had a need for it, we considered holding a special meeting for them. In January 1928 we rented some premises at Wen-teh Lane on Hardoon Road in Shanghai, and on February 1 we started the special meeting. The central theme of the messages was solely that of God's eternal purpose and the victory of Christ. We did not refer to other problems such as the truth as it concerned the church. There were twenty or thirty brothers and sisters who came from other places, but God illumined them and enabled them to see how they should walk along the path of life. They solved for themselves such problems as baptism, forsaking denominations, and other similar things. In the four years up until 1936, seven or eight hundred brothers and sisters were saved or revived in about ten meeting places north of the Yangtze River. In about the same number of meeting places in and around Ping-Yang and Tai-Shun, some four thousand were saved or revived. All this work was done by the Lord Himself, and He had been working for many years to bring it to pass.

After we moved to Wen-teh Lane in 1928, it was decided to continue publishing *The Present Testimony* since *The Christian* had ceased publication. In 1930 *Notes on Scriptural Messages* was published.

During those few years in Shanghai, our aim was to make people follow the Lord Himself, the teaching of the Scriptures, and the guidance of the Holy Spirit. We did not nor should we have expected anyone to give himself to us. This was not the so-called policy of exclusion, nor should it be taken to mean that we considered ourselves alone to be right; our only wish was to be loyal to the end. I wrote *The Spiritual Man* while I was ill; when it was completed, I became worse and was confined to bed practically all the time. Since the earthly house of my tabernacle was likely to collapse at any time, nothing worth mentioning was done during my first few years in Shanghai. It was in the following two years that things were actually started. In 1931 there was again a special meeting, of which the main message related to two enormous themes: the New Testament and the wisdom of God. At this meeting there were more brothers and sisters from other places.

GOD AS MY HEALER

When I first became aware of my illness in 1924, I was feeling feeble, there was pain in my chest, and I had a slight fever. I did not know what was wrong. Dr. H. S. Hwang said to me, "I know you have faith and that God can cure you, but allow me to examine you and diagnose your disease." After the examination he spoke to Brother Wong Teng-ming for some time in a very low voice. At first, even though I asked, they would not tell me the result of the examination. But when I informed them that I was not afraid, Dr. Hwang told me that I was afflicted with tuberculosis and that my condition was so serious that prolonged rest would be necessary.

I could not sleep that night; I did not want to meet the Lord without having completed my work. I was very depressed. I decided to go to the countryside for a rest and have more fellowship with the Lord. I asked the Lord, "What is Your will for me? If You wish me to lay down my life, I am not afraid to die." For half a year I could not grasp the Lord's will, but there was joy in my heart, and I believed the Lord could never be wrong. The many letters I received during this time did not convey encouragement or consolation; rather, they rebuked me for overworking and for not taking adequate care of my life. One brother reproached me by quoting Ephesians 5:29, "For no one ever hated his own flesh, but nourishes and cherishes it, even as Christ also the church." Brother Cheng Chi-kwei of Nanking invited me to his home where I could rest and at the same time help him translate Dr. C. I. Scofield's Bible correspondence course. At this time some thirty brothers and sisters came to me for fellowship. I spoke with them regarding the question of the church. I came to realize that God's hand was on me for the express purpose of turning me back to my first vision; otherwise, I would have ended up walking in the path of a revival preacher.

Day after day passed without my tuberculosis being cured. Though I exerted myself to write and to study the Bible, I found it exceedingly strenuous. I had a slight fever each afternoon, I could not sleep at night, and I frequently experienced night sweats. Upon being advised to take more rest, I replied, "I am afraid that I might rest to such a degree that I become rusty." I felt that even though I might not live long, I should believe that God would increase my strength and that I must work for Him. I asked the Lord concerning any unfinished work He had for me to do. Whatever He wanted me to do, I would ask Him to spare my life to do it; otherwise, I felt there was nothing upon earth worth living for. For awhile I was able to arise from bed, but eventually I could not even do that. On one occasion I was asked to conduct a gospel meeting. I exerted myself to arise and asked the Lord to strengthen me. While walking to the meeting, I was forced to lean against a lamp post every now and then for rest. Each time this happened I would say to the Lord, "It is worthwhile to die for You." Some brothers who knew that I had done this rebuked me for not sparing my health. To this I replied that I loved my Lord and would give up my life for Him.

After praying for over a month, I felt that I should write a book concerning what I had learned before God. My concept had been that one should not write books until he was old, but when I considered that I might be leaving this earth, I felt I should begin writing. I rented a small room in Wusih, Kiangsu province, where I shut myself up and spent my days writing. At that time my disease became so aggravated that I could not even lie down. While writing I sat on a chair with a high back and pressed my chest against the desk to alleviate the pain. Satan said to me, "Since you will soon be dying, why not die in comparative comfort rather than in pain?" I retorted, "The Lord wants me just like this; get out of here!" It took four months to complete the three volumes of *The Spiritual Man*. The writing of this book was a real labor of blood, sweat, and tears. I despaired of life, yet God's grace brought me through. After completing each time of writing, I would say to myself, "This is my last testimony to the church." Though the writing was done in the midst of all sorts of difficulties and hardships, I felt that God was unusually near to me. Some felt God was ill-treating me. Brother Cheng wrote saying, "You are exerting yourself to the uttermost; some day you will regret it." I replied, "I love my Lord and I would live for Him."

I wrote *The Spiritual Man* during my long illness. When it was ready for publication, about four thousand dollars were needed. Since there were no means on hand, I asked God to fill the need. Only four co-workers knew of this need. No one else knew. Before long the Lord provided four hundred dollars, and we entered into a contract with a printer to commence printing the book. It was agreed that should we fail to pay the subsequent installments, we would not only forfeit the cash down payment of four hundred dollars, but we would also pay for the default. We therefore prayed concerning this matter with one accord. At that time I was still confined to bed. Whenever the printer came for his payment, the Lord had always provided us with the means. Seeing that we were able to maintain good faith, the printer said, "No one but you church people make payments so punctually."

Following the publication of the book, I prayed, "Now let Your servant depart in peace." At the same time my disease worsened. I could not sleep peacefully at night, and when I awoke I turned incessantly from side to side. Physically, I was a bag of bones. I had night sweats, and my voice became hoarse. People had trouble hearing me speak, even when they placed their ear to my mouth. Several sisters took turns waiting upon me, one of whom was a veteran nurse. Whenever she saw me, she would weep. She testified, "I have seen many patients, but I have never seen one whose condition was as pitiful as his. I am afraid that he can live only three or four more days." When someone told me of this, I said, "Let this be my end. I realize I am going to die soon." One brother telegraphed the churches in various places, telling them there was no more hope for me and that they need pray for me no more.

One day I asked God, "Why are You calling me away so soon?" I confessed my trespasses before God, fearing that I might have been unfaithful concerning some matter. At the same time I told God that I had no faith. On that same day I devoted myself to fasting and praying and presented myself to Him once more. I told Him that I would do nothing but what He assigned me. From morning until three o'clock in the afternoon I fasted. At the same time the co-workers earnestly prayed together for me in Sister Ruth Lee's home. As I prayed to God to grant me faith, He spoke His words to me, words which I could never forget. The first sentence was, "The just shall live by faith" (Rom. 1:17). The second sentence was, "By faith you stand" (2 Cor. 1:24). The third sentence was, "We walk by faith" (2 Cor. 5:7). These words filled me with great joy, for the Bible says, "All things are possible to him who believes" (Mark 9:23). I immediately thanked and praised God because He had given me His words. I believed that God had cured me.

The test came immediately. The Bible says, "By faith you stand," but I was still lying in bed. A conflict arose in my mind: Should I get up and stand or remain lying down? We all know that human beings love themselves and consider it more comfortable to die in bed than to die standing. Then the word of God manifested its power, and ignoring all else, I put on my clothing, clothing which I had not worn for a hundred and seventy-six days. As I left the bed to stand, I perspired so profusely that it was as though I had been soaked through with rain. Satan said to me, "Are you trying to stand when you can't even sit up?" I retorted, "God told me to stand," and I rose to my feet. Being again in a cold sweat, I nearly fell down. I kept repeating, "Stand by faith, stand by faith!" I then walked a few steps to get my trousers and socks. After putting on my trousers, I sat down. No sooner was I seated than the word of God came to me that I should not only

stand by faith but also walk by faith. I felt that the ability
to rise and walk a few steps to get my trousers and socks
was already something marvelous. How could I expect to walk
further? "Where do You want me to go?" I asked God. He
answered, "Go downstairs to Sister Lee's home at number 215." A number of brothers and sisters had been fasting
and praying for me there for two or three days.

Walking within the room might be all right, I thought,
but how could I walk downstairs? I prayed to God, "Oh God,
I can stand by faith, and by faith I am also able to walk
downstairs!" Immediately, I went to the door leading to the
staircase and opened it. I tell you honestly that when I stood
at the top of the staircase it seemed to me to be the tallest
staircase I had ever seen in my life. I said to God, "If You
tell me to walk I will do so, even if I die as a result of the
effort." But I continued, "Lord, I cannot walk. I pray that You
will support me with Your hand while I am walking." With
one hand holding onto the rail, I descended step by step.
Again I was in a cold sweat. As I walked down the stairs, I
continued to cry out, "Walk by faith, walk by faith!" With
each step down, I prayed, "Oh Lord, it is You who enable me
to walk." While descending those twenty-five steps, it seemed
I was walking hand in hand with the Lord in faith.

Upon reaching the bottom of the stairway, I felt very
strong and went quickly to the rear door. I opened the door
and headed straight for Sister Lee's home. I said to the Lord,
"From now on, I will live by faith and will no longer be an
invalid." I knocked at the door just as Peter did in Acts
12:12-17, but without Rhoda to open the door. When the door
was opened and I entered the house, seven or eight brothers
and sisters gazed at me. They were speechless and motionless.
For about an hour everyone sat quietly as if God had appeared
among men. I also sat there full of thanksgiving and praise.
Then I related all that had happened in the course of my
being graciously healed. Exhilarated and jubilant in spirit,
we all praised God aloud for His wonderful work. That same
day we hired a car to go to Kiang-Wan in the suburbs to visit
Dora Yu, the famous woman evangelist. She was greatly
shocked to see me, for she had received recent news of my

imminent death. When I appeared, I was looked upon as one who had been raised from the dead. That was another occasion of joyful thanksgiving and praise before the Lord. On the following Sunday, I spoke on the platform for three hours.

About four years ago, I went to an auction at the house of a German doctor. Upon inquiring I found that this doctor was the one who had taken x-rays of my chest many years ago. He had taken three pictures and told me that there was no hope. When I asked him to take another picture, he said that there was no further need. He then showed me another person's chest x-ray and said, "This person's condition was better than yours, yet he died at his home two weeks after this picture was taken. Don't come to see me anymore; I don't want to make money out of you." When I heard this, I went home extremely disappointed. Then, four years ago, I read an advertisement in the newspaper concerning the auction of a building and furniture of a certain famous German doctor who had died. When I discovered that this doctor was the one who had taken x-rays of my chest many years ago, I lifted up my hands to praise the Lord. I said, "This doctor has died. He said that I would die soon, but now he is dead. The Lord has shown me His grace." Under the Lord's blood, I said, "This doctor, who was stronger than I, has died, but I have been healed by the Lord and am still alive." On that day I bought many things from his house for memorial.

GUIDANCE FOR WORK

From the time I was bedridden by illness until the time I was healed by God, I was being shown more clearly the kind of work God wanted me to do. This consists of the following four aspects:

Literary Work

Before I became ill, I not only visited various places to conduct special meetings, but I also had a great ambition to compose a good comprehensive commentary. I intended to devote much energy, time, and money in writing a large commentary consisting of about a hundred volumes. After completing *The Spiritual Man,* which I began in Nanking when I became ill, I realized that the task of expounding the Scriptures was not for me. However, since that time I have frequently met with temptation in this respect. After my illness, God revealed to me that the central point of the messages He gave me was not for expounding the Scriptures, preaching the ordinary gospel, paying attention to prophecies, or anything outward, but for laying stress on the living word of life. For this reason I felt I should resume publishing *The Present Testimony* to assist God's children in spiritual life and warfare. Each age has a unique truth especially needed in that time. For us, living in the last days, there must also be some truth which we especially need. By means of *The Present Testimony* the testimony for the truth of the present age was borne. I am profoundly convinced that the present is the preparatory period. Children of God will be reaped, but they have to become ripe first (Mark 4:29). The time for us to be caught up is full; whether or not the church is ready is the most vital problem. God's aim today is to expedite building up the Body of His Son, which is the church. As it is said in the Scripture: "That He might sanctify her, cleansing her by the washing of the water in the word, that He might present the church to Himself glorious" (Eph. 5:26-27), so that the enemy might be quickly destroyed to usher in the kingdom. I humbly hope that I may, in the hand of the Lord, have a little share in this glorious work. All that I have written has but one aim, which is that the reader will, in the new creation, give himself wholly to God and become a useful person in His hands. Now I wholeheartedly commit my writings, my readers, and myself to God, who preserves men forever, and hope that His Spirit will guide me into all His truths.

Conducting Overcomers' Meetings

God has shown me that in every local church a group of overcomers should be raised up (as those mentioned in Revelation 2 and 3) to be the Lord's witnesses. For this reason, every year an overcomer conference has been held to faithfully deliver the messages that God has given me.

Building Up Local Churches

When the Lord called me to serve Him, the prime object was not for me to hold revival meetings so that people might hear more scriptural doctrines, nor for me to become a great evangelist. The Lord revealed to me that He wanted to build up local churches in other localities to manifest Himself, to bear testimony of unity on the ground of locality so that each saint might perform his duty in the church and live the church life. God wants not merely individual pursuit of victory or spirituality, but a corporate, glorious church presented to Himself.

Training Young People

If the return of the Lord should be delayed, it will be necessary to raise up a number of young people to continue the testimony and the work for the following generations. Many co-workers have already prayed concerning this matter with the hope of providing a suitable place for the purpose of training young people. My thought is not to establish a seminary or a Bible institute, but to have young people staying together to live the Body life and practice the spiritual life. In such a place they would receive training for the purpose of edification, by learning to read the Scripture, to pray, and to build up a good character. On the negative side, there would be training for the purpose of learning how to deal with sin, the world, the flesh, and the natural life. At a suitable time, the young people would return to their respective churches in various places to be tempered together with other saints to serve the Lord in the church. I have purchased over ten acres of land at Chenru, in the suburbs of Shanghai. Planning for building on that site is in progress, and before long, young people will be able to go there for training.

In the future my personal burden and work will generally comprise these four aspects. May all the glory be to the Lord. We have nothing at all in ourselves, and though we have done something, we admit to being useless and unprofitable servants.

CHAPTER THREE

THE THIRD TESTIMONY—
GIVEN ON OCTOBER 20, 1936

Scripture Reading: Acts 26:29

LIVING A LIFE OF FAITH

Having given two testimonies, I had no intention of giving any more. However, while I was praying, it seemed that the Lord wanted me to testify once again. Those who know me are aware that I seldom testify regarding my own affairs. It has been my observation that people often abuse others' testimonies, treating them as news for circulation. It is also true that some testimonies are not sufficiently founded. The third-heaven experience of the apostle Paul was not disclosed to others until after fourteen years. Regarding many spiritual testimonies, an appropriate length of time should be allowed to elapse before they are divulged. Many, however, would speak them forth not in fourteen years, but in fourteen days.

Matters concerning Money

The matter of money can be either a small or a big problem. When I began to serve the Lord, I was somewhat anxious about the question of my livelihood. Had I been a preacher in a denomination, I would have been on a large monthly salary. But since I was to walk in the Lord's way, I would only rely upon Him to support me; I could not depend upon a monthly salary. In the years 1921 and 1922, very few preachers in China lived in sole reliance on the Lord. It was difficult to find even two or three; the great majority lived on salary. At that time many preachers were not bold enough to devote their entire time to serving the Lord; they felt that if they were not receiving a regular salary, they would not know how to face a situation in which they had nothing to live on. I also had such thoughts. In China today [1936] there are approximately fifty brothers and sisters in fellowship with us who live by relying solely on the Lord. Such a situation is more common now than it was in 1922. Brothers and sisters in various places today also care for the workers more than before. I think that after ten years or so, brothers and sisters will show even greater concern for the need of the servants of the Lord. But it was not very common ten years ago.

Declaring to My Parents
My Desire to Live by Faith

I have pointed out in a previous testimony that after I was saved I continued to study in school and at the same time work for the Lord. One evening I spoke with my father concerning the matter of receiving financial assistance. I said, "After praying for several days, I feel that I must tell you that I will no longer spend your money. I appreciate that you have spent so much on me in accord with your sense of fatherly responsibility. But you will expect me to earn money in the future and support you in return, and I must tell you beforehand that since I am going to be a preacher, I will not be able to repay you in the future nor pay you interest. Even though I have not completed my studies, I wish to learn to depend solely upon God." When I said this, my father thought I was joking. However, from then on, when my mother would occasionally give me five or ten dollars, she would write on the envelope: "To Brother Nee To-sheng." She was not giving me money as a mother.

After I had expressed myself thus to my father, the devil came to tempt me by saying, "Such an act is very dangerous. Suppose one day you are unable to maintain your living and you again approach your father for money. Won't that be disgraceful? You have spoken to your father too soon; you should have waited until there was more progress in your work, until many people had been saved and you had many friends, before you began to live a life of faith." But thank the Lord, ever since I expressed my decision to discontinue receiving my father's support, I have never asked him for money.

LOOKING TO GOD FOR
SUSTENANCE WHILE WORKING

To the best of my knowledge, Sister Dora Yu was the only preacher at that time who did not receive a salary and who depended wholly upon God for her living. She was my spiritual elder sister, and we knew each other very well. She had many friends, Chinese and foreign, and the field of her work was very wide since she preached everywhere. But my condition was just the opposite; few cared for me, so I found it rather difficult. Yet when I looked to the Lord, He said to me, "If you cannot live by faith, you cannot work for Me." I knew that I needed living work and living faith to serve a living God. When once I found that there was only about ten dollars in my wallet, which before long would be fully spent, I suddenly recalled the widow of Zarephath, who had only a handful of meal in the barrel and a little oil in the cruse (1 Kings 17:12). There were not two handfuls of meal. I did not know by what means God sustained her, but I knew He had the means.

In 1921 two co-workers and I went to a place in Fukien province to preach, intending to go from there to another place. In my pocket were only four dollars, an insufficient amount for three bus tickets. But, thank the Lord, a brother gave us three tickets.

Again, at Kulangsu, in the south of Fukien province, my money was stolen from my pocket, so that I had no traveling expenses to return home. We were then staying in someone's house and preached once a day in a small chapel. We finished and were ready to leave. My two co-workers had money to return home, but mine had been stolen. (At that time each of us was spending his own money.) They made the decision to leave on the following day. When I heard this I was embarrassed, but I was not willing to borrow money from them. That evening I prayed to God, beseeching Him to provide the needed money for traveling expenses. Nobody knew this. That afternoon some people had come to speak with me about the Word, but I was in no mood to do so. At that time the devil came to tempt me and shake my faith, but I was firm in believing that God would not let me down.

I was then merely a youth, just embarking on serving the
Lord by faith; I had not yet learned the lesson of living by
faith. I continued praying to God that evening, thinking that
perhaps I had done something wrong. The devil said, "You
could ask the co-workers to buy your ticket, then repay them
when you reach the provincial capital." I did not accept this
suggestion and continued looking to God. When the time came
for us to leave, there was still no money in hand. I packed
my luggage as usual and hired a rickshaw. At that moment,
I recalled the story of a brother who had no train ticket when
the train was about to leave, but at that very instant, God
ordered someone to give him a ticket. We were all ready and
boarded the rickshaws, of which there were three. I took the
last one. When the rickshaw had been pulled about forty
yards, an old man in a long gown came from behind shouting,
"Mr. Nee, please stop!" I ordered the rickshaw boy to halt.
After handing me a parcel of food as well as an envelope,
the old man departed. I was then so grateful for God's
arrangement that my eyes were filled with tears. When I
opened the envelope, I found four dollars inside, just sufficient
for a bus ticket. The devil kept speaking to me, "Don't you
see how dangerous it is?" I replied, "I was indeed a little
anxious about it, but it is by no means dangerous, for God
has supplied my need in time." After arriving in Amoy,
another brother gave me a return ticket.

In 1923 Brother Weigh Kwang-hsi invited me to preach
in Kien-ou in the north of Fukien province. I had only about
fifteen dollars in my pocket, one-third of the traveling
expenses. I decided to leave on Friday evening and continued
my prayer on Wednesday and Thursday. The money, however,
did not come in. I prayed again Friday morning. Not only
was no money forthcoming, but also I had a feeling within
that I should give five dollars to a certain co-worker. I recalled
the Lord's words: "Give, and it will be given to you." I had
not been a money lover, but on that day I really loved money
and found it extremely difficult to give. I prayed to the Lord
again, "O Lord, if You really want me to give away five dollars,
I will," but I was still rather unwilling inwardly. I was
deceived by Satan into thinking that after praying I would

not have to give away the five dollars. That was the only time in my life that I shed tears over money. Eventually, I obeyed the Lord and gave the five dollars to that co-worker. After the money was given, I was filled with heavenly joy. When the co-worker asked why I gave him the money, I said, "You need not ask; you will know later."

Friday evening I prepared to begin my journey. I said to God, "Fifteen dollars was already insufficient, and You wanted me to give away five dollars. Won't the sum be even more inadequate? Now I don't know how to pray." I made up my mind to go first to Shui-Kow by steamer and then to Kien-ou by a small wooden boat. I spent only a little for the journey to Shui-Kow. As the steamer was about to arrive, I felt that if I would not pray according to my own concept, the result would be much better. So I said to the Lord, "I do not know how to pray; please do it for me." I added, "If You will not give me the money, please provide a boat for me with a little fare." When I arrived in Shui-Kow, many boatmen came to solicit business. One asked only seven dollars for my passage. This price was beyond expectation; the usual fare was several times more. I asked the boatman why his price was so low, and he replied, "This boat is hired by the magistrate, but I am allowed to take one passenger only for the space at the stern, so I do not care how much the fare is. But you have to provide your own food." Originally, I had fifteen dollars in my pocket. After giving five dollars to a co-worker and spending a few dimes for the journey by steamer, seven dollars for the small wooden boat, and a dollar or so for food, there was still a dollar thirty left when I reached Kien-ou. Thank the Lord! Praise Him that His ordering is always good.

After I completed my work at Kien-ou and was ready to return to Foochow, the problem arose again: I did not have sufficient funds for traveling expenses to return. I had decided to leave on the following Monday, so I continued praying until Saturday. This time I had a feeling of certainty in my heart, recalling that before I left Foochow, God had asked me to give five dollars to a co-worker, which I then begrudged giving. At that time I read Luke 6:38: "Give, and it will be given to you," and I laid hold of this sentence. I said to God, "Since

You have said this, I beseech You to provide me with the necessary money for traveling expenses according to Your promise."

On Sunday evening a British pastor, Mr. Philips, a true brother, assuredly saved and loving the Lord, asked Brother Weigh and me to dinner. At dinner Mr. Philips told me that he and his church had received great help through my messages, and they offered to be responsible for my traveling expenses both ways. I replied that there was already someone who had accepted this responsibility, meaning God. Then he said, "When you get back to Foochow, I will give you *The Dynamic of Service* written by Mr. Padget Wilkes, a gospel messenger greatly used by the Lord in Japan." I soon felt that I had missed a great opportunity; what I needed then was money for traveling expenses, not a book. I somewhat regretted that I had not accepted his offer. After dinner Brother Weigh and I returned home together. I had refused Mr. Philips's offer for my traveling expenses so that I might look solely to God for help; nevertheless, there was joy and peace in my heart. Brother Weigh was unaware of my financial situation. I had a slight thought of borrowing money from him for my expenses and then reimbursing him when I returned to Foochow, but God would not allow me to divulge this matter to him. I was under full conviction that God in heaven is forever dependable, and I wished to see how He was going to provide for me.

When I left the following day, I had only a few dollars in my pocket. Many brothers and sisters came to see me off, and some carried my luggage. While walking I prayed, "Lord, surely You wouldn't bring me here without taking me back." Halfway to the wharf, Mr. Philips sent someone with a letter. The letter read, "Though someone else has assumed the responsibility for your traveling expenses, I feel that I should have a share in your work here. Would it be possible for me, an aged brother, to have such a share? Please be good enough to accept this small sum for this purpose." After reading the letter, I felt I should accept the money, and I did. It was not only sufficient for my return expenses to Foochow, but also for printing one issue of *The Present Testimony*.

Upon my return to Foochow, the wife of the co-worker who received the five dollars said to me, "I have the feeling that when you left you did not have enough money yourself. Why did you suddenly give five dollars to my husband?" I then asked her what had occurred in connection with the five dollars, and she replied, "We had only one dollar left in the house on Wednesday, and that had been spent by Friday. On Friday we prayed all day. Afterwards my husband felt that he should go for a walk, and then he met you, and you gave him five dollars. The five dollars lasted us through five days; then God provided for us from another source." At this point she continued with tears, "If you had not given us the five dollars on that day, we would have suffered hunger. It does not matter that we suffer hunger, but what about God's promise?" Her testimony filled me with joy. The Lord had worked through me to supply their need with the five dollars. The Word of the Lord is indeed faithful: "Give, and it will be given to you."

This is the lesson I have learned in my life. I have now experienced that the less money I have in my hand, the more God will give. This is a difficult path to follow. Many people may feel that they are able to live the life of faith; but when the trial comes, they are in fear. Unless you can believe in the real and living God, I do not advise you to take this path. I can bear testimony today that God is the One who gives. To be sustained by means of ravens as Elijah was at his time is still possible today. I am going to mention something to you which you may find difficult to believe. It has been my experience that God's supply arrives when I have spent my last dollar. I have had fourteen years of experience. In each experience God wanted to get the glory for Himself. God has supplied all my needs and has not failed me once. Those who used to give do not do so now. There is a constant change of offerers; one lot of people replaces another. All this does not matter, for God in the highest is a living God. He never changes! I say this today for your benefit. I must say this that you may go straight forward in the path of living a life of faith. There are ten to twenty more cases like these that I have already related to you.

Concerning the matter of offering the Lord money, one ought to set aside a definite amount—a tithe of your income or half of your income—and put it in the hand of God. From her natural being, the widow who gave two half-farthings might have grudged doing so, but she was praised by the Lord. We have to be an example for others; we need not fear, for God will not fail. We should learn to love God, to believe Him, and to serve Him as is His due. We ought to thank Him and praise Him because of His unspeakable grace! Amen.

Looking to God for Sustenance for the Publication Work

Some people would never enter a meeting place to listen to the gospel. For this reason, in 1922 I began printing gospel tracts. The gospel must be delivered to them. After writing the tracts, I began praying and asking for provision for the printing and distribution expenses. God said to me, "If you wish Me to answer your prayer, you must first rid yourself of all hindrances." On the following Sunday, I preached on the theme, "Removal of All Hindrances." At that very time many people were criticizing the wife of one of my co-workers, who was a sister among us. After the meeting she stood at the door. When I entered the meeting to deliver the message, I looked at her and inwardly criticized her, considering others' criticism of her to be true. When I left the meeting hall after delivering the message, I greeted her. Later, when I again supplicated God for printing expenses, saying that I had removed all hindrances, God said to me, "What is the message which you have delivered? You have criticized that sister; that is a hindrance to prayer, a hindrance which you ought to deal with. You must go to her and confess your guilt." I replied, "It is not necessary to confess to others sins that are in the mind." God answered, "Yes, that is right, but your condition is different." Afterward, when I considered confessing to her and came face to face with the issue, I hesitated five times. Even though I wished to do it, I was concerned that she, who had always greatly admired me, would then despise me. I said to God, "If You order me to do anything else, I will do it, but I am unwilling to confess to her." I continued to ask

God for the printing expenses, but He would not listen to my reasoning. Rather, He insisted on my confessing. The sixth time, through the Lord's grace, I confessed to her. With tears we both confessed our faults and then forgave each other. We were filled with joy and thereafter loved each other all the more in the Lord.

Shortly after this, the postman delivered a letter containing fifteen U.S. dollars. The letter read, "I like to distribute gospel tracts and feel constrained to assist you in the matter of printing gospel tracts. Please accept my gift." As soon as all hindrances were removed, God answered my prayer. Thank the Lord! This was my first experience of God's answering my prayer in the matter of printing. We were then handing out more than a thousand tracts daily. Two or three million copies were printed and distributed annually to supply the churches in various places. In the few years after the publication work was begun, God always answered my prayers and supplied all our needs.

The Lord also wanted me to publish the magazine *The Present Testimony* and to give it out free of charge. At that time all spiritual periodicals throughout China were for sale; only what I published was free. The editing room where I wrote the manuscripts was a small cubicle. When the manuscripts were completed, they were sent to the press. When there were no funds available, I would pray to God for His provision for printing. When I considered what I was doing, I laughed because the manuscripts were being sent to the press without the necessary funds. As long as I live, I will never forget the time when I had no sooner finished laughing than there was a knock at the door. Upon opening the door, I saw a middle-aged woman who constantly came to the meetings but to whom my heart was unusually cool. She was wealthy, but she loved money and treated a dime as a dollar. I wondered how she could possibly be the one who would give money for printing the magazine. Then I asked her why she had come. She replied, "About an hour ago I began feeling inwardly uneasy. When I prayed to God, He told me that I am not like a Christian, for I have never done well in the matter of offering, and that I love money too much. I asked Him what He wanted me to do, and He said, 'You should offer some money for the use of My work.'" Then she took out thirty silver dollars and placed them on the table, saying, "Spend it on whatever you feel the need is." Then as I looked at the table, I saw two things, the manuscripts and the money. I thanked the Lord without thanking her. She left, and I went immediately to the printers to negotiate the printing. The money she had given was sufficient to print fourteen hundred copies of the magazine. Others gave money for the packing expenses and postage. Now about seven thousand copies of each issue are being printed. All the finances required are provided by God at the right time and in the way I have been relating. I have never solicited contributions from anyone. At times people have even begged me to accept money. In all of these matters I have been looking solely to Him.

ACCEPTING MONEY ON CHRIST'S BEHALF

If one fails in dealing properly with monetary matters, he will also certainly fail in many other things. We must single-mindedly look to God and never do anything which will bring disgrace to the Lord. When people give us money, we accept it on behalf of Christ, and we must never ask people for any favors. Thanks be to God that after I told my parents I was not going to spend their money any longer, I was still able to study at school for two more years. Though I did not know where the sustenance came from, whenever there was a need, God certainly provided. Sometimes the situation looked really difficult, yet God never let me down. We often place our hope in other people, but God does not want us to look to others. We should learn a lesson: spend as we receive, and never be like the Dead Sea, with inlets but without a single outlet. We ought to be like the river Jordan, with inlets on the one side and outlets on the other. The Levites in the Old Testament were those who devoted themselves to serving God, and they too had to offer their tithes.

A LETTER
FROM BROTHER WATCHMAN NEE
TO THE COMPILER
MARCH 10, 1950

Dear Brother Weigh,

I have long been thinking of writing to you, but I have put it off lest my thoughts were not sufficiently mature to do so. However, I think it is now the opportune time. I hope you will humbly place this before God.

I am afraid the difficulties of the churches in Hong Kong and Canton will be rather enormous, namely (a) among co-workers and (b) in the church. I hope what I am going to say below will, through the grace of the Lord, help towards changing the situation there.

(1) Those who are leaders ought to learn to love others, to think on their behalf, to take care of them, to deny oneself for their sake, and to give them all one has. If one cannot deny himself on account of others, it would be impossible to guide people along the spiritual path. Learn to give others what you have even if you feel as if you have nothing. Then the Lord will start pouring down His blessing.

(2) The inner strength of a worker should measure up to the outward work. There should not be any overstrain, overreaching, uneasiness, scantiness, tension, lack of over-flowing, human plans, or going ahead of the Lord. All these are undesirable conditions. If one is inwardly abundant, whatever is emanating from him is like the flowing of a stream, and there is no overstrain on his part. You must really be a spiritual man; you should not merely act like one.

(3) Learn to listen to others in connection with your work. The teaching in Acts 15 is to listen, that is, to listen to the views of all brothers because the Holy Spirit may speak through them. Be very careful lest in refusing to listen to

the voice of the brothers you may not hear the voice of the Holy Spirit. All the co-workers and elders ought to sit down to listen to them. Give them unrestricted chances to speak. Be gentle, be broken, and be prepared to listen.

(4) The difficulty with many people is their being unbroken. They may have heard about being "broken," but its significance eludes them. If one is broken, he will not attempt to arrive at his own decision regarding business matters or teaching, will not claim to understand people or to be capable of doing things, will not venture to assume authority or to impose his own authority upon others, and will not take the liberty to criticize brothers or to deal with them presumptuously. A brother who is broken will not try to defend himself, and there is nothing he needs to look back to.

(5) There should be no tension in meetings or in the church. Regarding church business, learn not to do too much yourself. Distribute the business among others and make them learn to use their own discretion in making decisions. You should first brief them on the fundamental principles to follow and ascertain afterwards whether they have acted accordingly. It is wrong to do too much personally. Avoid showing yourself in excess in meetings, otherwise the brothers may feel that you are monopolizing. Learn to place trust in the brothers and divide it among them.

(6) The Spirit of God cannot be coerced in the church. You have to be submissive to Him; otherwise, once He stops anointing, the church will feel tired or possibly even bored. If your spirit is strong, it will sweep over and overwhelm the audience within ten minutes; if it is weak, even shouting some threatening words and spending a longer time will not help and may even be harmful.

(7) In delivering a message, do not make it too long or too elaborate; otherwise, the spirit of the saints may tend to feel bored. Do not include superficial thoughts or base statements in the contents of your message; avoid childish examples as well as those reasons which are so common that people will consider them childish. Learn to finish delivering the essence within half an hour. Do not think that, when you

yourself enjoy your message, the words are necessarily those of God.

(8) The temptation often encountered at a prayer meeting is to deliver a message or to speak at length. A prayer meeting should be devoted to praying; too much talking will make the conscience feel heavy with the result that the meeting becomes a failure.

(9) The work at Kuling, Fukien, in 1948 was an exceptional case. Workers should learn a lot before getting into a position where they deal with problems or persons. With inadequate learning, insufficient knowledge, incomplete brokenness, and unreliable judgment, one will be incompetent to deal with others. Do not jump to conclusions; even when one is about to do something, he should do it in fear and trembling. Do not treat spiritual matters lightly. Learn in the heart.

(10) Learn not to trust your own judgments only. What is considered right may not be so; what is regarded wrong may not be wrong. If one is determined to learn humbly, it will take at least a few years to complete. Therefore, for the present, you ought not to have too much confidence in yourself or be too definite about your way of thinking.

(11) It would be a dangerous thing for people in the church to follow your decisions before you reach the state of maturity. The Lord will work on you to deal with your thoughts and to break you before you can understand the will of God and thus be His authority. Authority is based on the knowledge of the Lord's will. Where the Lord's will and purpose are not manifest, there is no authority.

(12) The capacity of a servant of God should be constantly expanded by Him. I think He is now doing it; you need not look inward, since this will make you disheartened. God may wish you to assume the responsibility of leadership. As to the work in Hong Kong, it is possible that some brothers will feel led to join it. I think we ought to have rest in the matter.

Yours in the Lord,
Nee To-sheng (Watchman Nee)